Original title:
The Necklace's Secret

Copyright © 2025 Creative Arts Management OÜ
All rights reserved.

Author: Lucas Harrington
ISBN HARDBACK: 978-1-80586-166-9
ISBN PAPERBACK: 978-1-80586-638-1

Facades of Fortune

A trinket glimmers, oh so fine,
Crafty smiles, they intertwine.
Her laughter dances, a feigned delight,
While dreams of riches take flight.

In borrowed gowns, she struts around,
A queen of fools, in joy she's drowned.
But behind each sparkle, a truth does hide,
That fortunes flip like a fickle tide.

Silent Betrayals

In crowded rooms, the whispers roam,
With every glance, she feels at home.
A friend applauds, her pricy charm,
Yet laugh's a cover—an unseen harm.

For every jewel that catches the eye,
A tale of woe treads nigh.
She wears her pride like feathered hair,
Unknowing of the shadows laid bare.

A Dance with Vanity

At splendid balls, she twirls with glee,
Eyes on her gem, the world to see.
But cringes echo with every spin,
As whispers mock the joy within.

Each joyous twirl hides a twist of fate,
For vanity wears a silly gait.
While laughter rings, a cost is high,
For gems can blind, 'neath a sapphire sky.

Beneath the Glimmer

With every shimmer comes a jest,
A secret wish that's not the best.
She struts about in borrowed light,
While shadows chuckle at her plight.

The diamond's gleam, oh, what a tease,
Yet chases hope like buzzing bees.
For under glimmers, the truth may squirm,
In folly's dance, we twist and turn.

Echoes of Enchantment

In a box of treasures, a sparkly find,
A dazzling piece that was one of a kind.
Worn to the ball with flair and delight,
Lost in the night, what a comical sight!

The search was frantic, the friends all laughed,
"We'll find that gem, we'll do our craft!"
But under the couch, all they did see,
Was a cat with a collar, looking oh so free.

Hues of Heartache

A shiny dream wrapped in a tale,
Set for the dance, but oh! She was pale.
With one swift move and a curious spin,
Now it's gone - well, didn't that begin?

Her heart went thump, her eyes did roll,
"A night on the town!" was their silly goal.
But on the way home, a neighbor did shout,
"Did you lose something? It's all over the route!"

Shadows Behind the Shine

With glimmering hopes, she twirled and posed,
But in the moonlight, the truth was exposed.
A sparkly surprise turned into a fuss,
For what was a jewel became a big plus!

Laughter erupted, as friends gathered near,
"What's that glint? Is it Google, my dear?"
Turns out it was just a shiny old lid,
Now fashion questions on what she did!

Glimmers of Regret

In dream of shine, her plans took flight,
But alas, oh dear! No jewel in sight.
With giggles and gasps, she took the stage,
But her treasure was lost, oh what a cage!

They searched and they searched until they were sore,
"Check in your purse, or maybe that drawer!"
Finding the truth made everyone smile,
It was tucked in her bra, oh the style!

Threads of a Dream

In a box of glitter, she found a treasure,
Hoping to wear it, oh what a pleasure!
But when she grabbed it, it slipped and fell,
Bounced off the floor like a baby gazelle.

Strutting in style, she felt like a queen,
With laughter around, it was quite a scene.
Yet the sparkle she wore was a hilarious sight,
A paper-made broach that shone oh so bright!

Whispers of Elegance

A soirée where whispers danced in the air,
She slipped on her bling, without a care.
The clinks and the clatters rang loud like a bell,
Her purse was so heavy, oh what the hell!

As she reached for her drink, a deer in the wild,
Her jewels all jangled, manners defiled.
Yet she twirled and she laughed, a lighthearted twist,
In the whirlwind of chaos, she couldn't resist!

Shimmering Illusions

With jewels that sparkled, she danced on the floor,
Every twirl and spin got her wanting more.
But a snag on her dress, oh dear what a mess,
Her jewels then conspired, causing distress.

In a flash, they flew—their own little show,
Hitching rides on the heads of friends in a row.
She giggled and chased, in a dainty ballet,
A slapstick performance that stole the day!

Treasures Unrevealed

In the depths of a closet, she found quite a stash,
Something shiny and bold, oh what a flash!
Thinking luck was with her, she donned it with flair,
But it turned out to be a dog's toy, oh beware!

With sparkles and glimmers that laughed in delight,
She paraded the street without spot of fright.
But the dog chased her down, a sight so absurd,
As she ran with the squeaker, she surely concurred!

Timeless Treasures

In a box, shiny jewels hide,
But the truth, she cannot abide.
Wearing diamonds, oh what a show,
Yet it's plastic, this we both know.

With every twinkle, a giggle sneaks,
A faux fortune, her heart it tweaks.
Guests all swoon, gasping with glee,
While she's yes, lying, just slightly carefree.

At the party, her sparkle shines bright,
But behind closed doors, what a fright!
A wrinkled dress and a pouting pout,
She'll wear fake treasures and laugh about!

In the end, when the dawn is near,
She'll find real joy in laughter sheer.
For treasures do laugh, and that's the jest,
True wealth is the moment we cherish best.

Fragile Facades

A tale of glam and bright charades,
Wearing shimmer but dodging blades.
With each step, a crack might sound,
But who needs truth when jesting's found?

She walks with grace, a royal's blush,
While her gems are just paper-hush.
When calling cards from friends arrive,
She flaunts her fake gems, feeling alive!

Her mirror winks, "Oh, what a flair!"
They sparkle and gleam, but do they care?
She'll tell them tales of diamond skies,
While hiding the truth behind her lies.

But laughter's gold and twinkling cheer,
Shimmers brighter than any veneer.
In the end, who needs a crown?
When humor's the treasure that won't back down!

Glistening Facade

At a party, she dazzled in style,
With a twinkle and grin, she walked a mile.
Her laughter rang out, a joyous parade,
While whispers around said, 'What a charade!'

Borrowed treasure, oh such a sight,
A sparkly show, pure delight.
But under the glow of the bright chandelier,
She knew in her heart, it was all just veneer.

A Glimpse of Grandeur

In a gown that could make the angels weep,
She drank up attention, a secret to keep.
With jewels that sparkled from head to toe,
But the truth of her story, few seemed to know.

"What's the catch?" the eager crowd would ask,
As she played her part, an unattended task.
Her grin was a riddle, a puzzle unspun,
While the night spun around, oh what fun!

The Weight of Wonder

She twirled and she swayed, feeling so grand,
Every jest a treasure, every joke well planned.
But a tug on her earlobe turned laughter to dread,
As the shiny bauble slipped and then fled.

"Oh no!" she declared, with a dramatic flair,
Her mystery prize vanished into thin air.
The crowd held their breath, eyes wide in surprise,
While she searched for the sparkle, where could be the prize?

Unraveling Mysteries

As the clock struck twelve, the fun met its limit,
The bravest of souls took a peek at her gimmick.
A stumble, a fumble, then laughter erupted,
Her dazzling facade, somehow corrupted.

With a wink and a giggle, she set them all straight,
"My charm's not just bling, it's truly first rate!"
In a world full of sparkle, she found her true worth,
The joy in the folly, her own source of mirth.

A Heart in Chains

A shiny gem, she lost a lot,
Yet claimed she wore a golden plot.
With mischief twinkling in her eye,
She swirled that tale – oh me, oh my!

Her friends all gasped, their jaws did drop,
As tales of riches made them hop.
But truth was stuck in tangled dread,
How could she face her debt instead?

The Dazzling Mask

A party came, and there she shone,
With a mask to hide the truth she'd known.
Her bling was bold, like stars at night,
But woes beneath kept her uptight.

With every laugh, her pulse would race,
What if they knew her hidden face?
Yet sparkling tales brought joyous cheer,
While secrets played, they'd never hear.

Secrets Beneath the Surface

She told her pals of treasures rare,
While hiding fabric ripped with care.
Each story spun, more grand, more bright,
Yet bubbles formed, she'd soon take flight.

As laughter rang, her heart would pound,
Would they suspect? Would truth be found?
But charm and whimsy won the day,
As outward glitz held woes at bay.

Dreams Adorned

In dreams adorned, her wishes danced,
Around their heads her luck enhanced.
Yet in the dark, the truth would creep,
Her fortune's glow was not too deep.

While in her dreams, she'd wear a crown,
In waking world, she'd just frown down.
But humor grasped her with a tease,
As funny tales brought all to knees.

The Glimpse of Deceit

In a shiny shop, a glimmer caught,
She thought she'd found the treasure sought.
With borrowed gems, she danced in glee,
But oh, the truth was a sight to see!

Mirror reflection, oh so grand,
Yet it slipped right through her hand.
Fell laughter echoed from the crowd,
As her pretense crumbled loud!

A Radiant Mirage

A shimmer here, a sparkle there,
With every glance, she played the flaire.
But behind each shine, a twinge of doubt,
Just a plastic gem, she found out!

At the gala, she took the stage,
In her jewels, she turned the page.
But as she twirled, the necklace broke,
And laughter spilled like a funny joke!

Adorned in Shadows

In shadows deep, her treasures gleamed,
With every step, her envy streamed.
She wore a crown, but no real gold,
A story of fraud, all too bold!

As she laughed, a chain did snap,
Oh dear, what a comical trap!
Friends all gasped, then burst with cheer,
For the faux jewels became quite dear!

Echoes of Envy

With every flicker, she strutted proud,
Around her neck, a shiny shroud.
Oh how the others stared in awe,
At jewels that were nothing but pure flaw!

When she tripped and all went wrong,
The laughter rose, a merry song.
Her grand facade, a playful tease,
Left everyone rolling, if you please!

The Price of Possession

In a shop with jewels so bright,
She glimpsed a spark that felt just right.
A shiny trinket, oh what a sight,
She tossed her coin, her heart took flight.

Yet in her haste, she missed the cue,
A fortune spent on what? A dew?
With laughter shared, the truth flew through,
A little gem, but none too new.

Secrets Beneath the Surface

In whispers soft, the rumors played,
Of treasures found, and debts delayed.
A mirror cracked, reflections frayed,
What hid beneath? The charade stayed.

Old coats and hats piled high with pride,
Where jokes and laughter often bide.
The secret kept, with hearts allied,
For in the mess, the fun's the ride.

Treasures of the Heart

A heart of gold wrapped tight in glee,
With stories shared, like cups of tea.
They laughed aloud, so carefree,
For riches found are not in spree.

In lunch or chats, the wealth was streamed,
In bonds of warmth, they often dreamed.
The real gold shone, or so it seemed,
In every hug where laughter gleamed.

The Cost of Splendor

A gala night with lights aglow,
She wore a dress, a vibrant show.
Yet every twirl, a price to sow,
As toes got stepped on, oh no, no!

The splendor made the crowd admire,
But tangled hair sparked a new fire.
In giggles loud, they climbed higher,
What joy emerged from mishap dire!

Mysteries in the Moonlight

In the dim light, secrets glow,
A lost gem on a housecat's toe.
Chasing shadows like a silly fool,
Who needs jewels when you own a pool?

Laughter echoed in the night,
As we danced, what a sight!
The real treasure? A funny friend,
With whom the joy shall never end.

Serpents of Splendor

A serpent draped in dazzling charms,
Slithered by, igniting alarms.
Oh, how it sparkled, oh what flair,
Is it jewelry? Or a fashion scare?

Amidst the giggles, it coils around,
Tickling everyone on the ground.
With every twist, a hearty laugh,
Turns a night into a silly gaffe.

Unraveled Grace

A lady's charm, so poised and grand,
Wore pearls like a lucky band.
But in a hiccup, they tumbled free,
Like popcorn dancing on a spree!

Rolling and bouncing, what a scene!
They glimmered like stars on a routine.
Grace is cute, and spills are fun,
When hilarity's just begun!

Aura of Ambiguity

In the closet lurked a delight,
A quirky hat, oh what a sight!
With feathers and beads galore,
It made us laugh, but oh, what for?

Uncertainty wrapped in every fiber,
Is it a joke or just a briber?
In the end, we wear it proud,
And dance together, laugh aloud!

Illusions of Elegance

She wore a gem, oh what a sight,
But it sparkled only in the light!
Fooling friends with every glance,
While her wallet did the funny dance.

In search of class, she borrowed flair,
With borrowed jewels beyond compare.
Yet at night, she'd clutch her chest,
As her heart said, 'Was that a jest?'

A Jewel's Whisper

A trinket bright, the envy around,
But what was lost could soon be found.
As laughter echoed, tales amassed,
Of how that bauble might not last.

'Oh darling, it's unique!' she'd tease,
While everyone saw the cheap knock knees.
With each faux-glimmer came a wink,
As she jittered, forgotten pink drink.

Ties That Bind

A clasp of pearls that made her grin,
But under the surface, lies begin.
She tied her fate to shining glee,
Yet tripped on strings of irony.

Her friends all laughed, oh what a show,
For no one knew the truth below.
With every party she'd flaunt, a jest,
Was she just the wearer or the best-dressed?

Veils of Deceit

A shiny ring to catch the eye,
But all it held was a sly lie.
She smiled wide, the truth concealed,
While in the shadows, secrets squealed.

Every glance brought squeaky laughs,
As fate conspired, like silly drafts.
And when asked, she'd bat her lash,
'It's just a thrill, not a stash!'

Reflections of Worth

In the mirror, I preen and pose,
Wearing baubles that nobody knows.
I feel like a queen, my self-worth is high,
Yet it's just plastic, oh me, oh my!

With diamonds that sparkle, I strut like a cat,
But underneath, it's just an old hat.
Friends shout, 'Is that real? What a find!'
I just laugh and pretend I'm so blind!

They say I'm a flasher, I've got a flair,
While I'm dreaming of riches, they just stare.
But when I trip up, oops! Down I go,
My 'jewels' just clattering, stealing the show!

In the end, it's the laughter I cherish the most,
As I strut around like a glamorous ghost.
With echoes of laughter, I simply say,
Who needs real gems when humor's the way?

Silken Chains

Oh, look at my chains, they shimmer and shine,
Tangled up in giggles, feeling divine.
They tug and they pull, oh, what a scene,
Wrapped in my own web, like a fashion queen!

In a silk scarf, I get all tied up,
Struggling for grace, oh, fill my cup!
Friends roll their eyes, 'You're a sight to behold!'
As I fumble around, acting so bold!

Once in a while, I wear things so bright,
It's hard to whine when I'm wrapped up tight.
A slip and a slide becomes a bold dance,
I laugh at my fate, who needs a romance?

So here's to the chains that make me unique,
In my tangled-up world, I'm laughter's sweet peak.
With silk that can trip me, I'm proud to say,
Life is a circus, come laugh and play!

Underneath the Sparkle

Beneath all the sparkle, a story unfolds,
Of dishes and dinners, and fortunes of old.
Here in my drawer, I find things galore,
Plastic and tin, treasures I adore!

With my sequined dress, I'm ready to roam,
Dancing in kitchens, pretending it's home.
The glimmer confuses, it twinkles so bright,
Yet really now, it's just a wild night!

Jewels burst out laughing at jokes that they weave,
As I slip on my shoes, you'd hardly believe.
With laughter as thick as the sparkling gleam,
They wink and they nod, oh, how fun it seems!

So here's to the fun that we bring every week,
With sparkles and laughter, that's all that we seek.
Hidden beneath all the glitz and the glow,
Are friends that I cherish, our laughter will flow!

A Gem's Dilemma

A gem in the box, snug and tight,
Wonders if it'll ever get to see light.
Shiny and pretty, more than a trinket,
Yet stuck in this drawer, it starts to rethink it.

"Oh, what a dilemma! Am I just for show?
Or a heart in a party?" It starts to glow.
While people parade, this gem starts to pout,
"Put me on something, let's dance all about!"

But then it remembers, 'I'm just a cheap deal,
What if they laugh? What's the big reveal?'
So it stays in the dark, feeling glum in its space,
Imagining sparkles that light up the place.

Yet when the door opens, and a hand reaches in,
The gem takes a breath, ready to grin.
Who cares how I sparkle, or what value I hold?
It's laughter and love that make me feel bold!

The Lure of Opulence

In sparkling gems, she took delight,
A simple girl, with dreams so bright.
She donned the pearls with flair and grace,
And danced around with a shining face.

But oh! The weight was more than glass,
A charming curse of bling and sass.
She tripped on lace, her heels a fright,
Made quite a scene in the moonlight.

Friends gasped, their laughs like musical chairs,
As pearls went flying, through the air!
A dazzling flop, a moment grand,
She learned the truth was light and bland.

So back she wandered, to simpler days,
With laughter echoing, in silly ways.
Her heart was rich, her joy set free,
Opulence can't buy such glee!

Echoes of Desire

With glittering dreams, she sought her fate,
A fanciful wish, but oh, so late!
In towering heels and taffeta bright,
She strutted out, ready for the night.

But fate had plans, as it does, you see,
Her skirt got caught, oh dear me!
A rip, a tear, and the world did pause,
She stood half-dressed, a stricken cause.

Laughter erupted, a chorus divine,
As she wiggled and jiggled, still trying to shine.
Yet strutting with style, her spirit ablaze,
She laughed along, spinning in a craze.

In the echoes of wish and whimsical glee,
She found that joy's spark was fashion's decree.
For riches may fade, and glam may impair,
But a heart full of laughs is beyond compare!

Gilded Trappings

In a costume ball, with feathers and gold,
She dressed to impress, or so she was told.
With rings on her fingers, and bells on her toes,
She twirled on the floor, in her gilded clothes.

But whoops, oh dear! Her dress gave a fight,
It snagged on a chair, what a comical sight!
With every spin, the fabric would burst,
Leaving behind what once was a first.

The crowd roared with laughter, oh what a scene!
As she hobbled and jiggled in sheer rhinestone sheen.
Gilded trappings can be such a snare,
Yet her chuckles were brighter than diamonds laid bare.

So while she was shunned for her fashion's faux pas,
She found that her laughter was truly the star.
For in woven tales, and folly's embrace,
She learned it's the joy that should take center space!

The Unseen Burden

She wore a crown, so opulent and bold,
A visage of royalty, or so she was sold.
But underneath it all, oh what a twist,
The weight of her jewels could not be missed.

At parties she sparkled, the envy of all,
Yet she tripped and stumbled, with every enthrall.
The tiara slipped, what a comical scene,
As she fumbled and fished, like a fish out of sheen.

Each glance, a chuckle, as tales were spun,
Her rhinestone dreams crumbling, yet still she'd run.
With laughter that echoed through halls, oh so wide,
She managed to giggle, though her jewels just cried.

For while she grumbled of burdens she bore,
She knew in her heart, that it's laughs we adore.
So she twirled again, in her gilded array,
Finding lightness in laughter, come what may!

The Pendant's Paradox

In a box, she found a gem,
Thought she'd strut like them,
But oh, what a surprise there,
A fake, with no flair!

She wore it with elation,
A grand masquerade sensation,
But it slipped right off her neck,
A fast-paced, funny wreck!

Friends all laughed, what a sight,
Chasing jewels in broad daylight,
Like magpies lost in dreams,
Life's not always what it seems!

She learned to wear a grin,
Now it's laughter, not the win,
In a world of glitzy schemes,
Reality burst all her dreams!

Veil of Glamour

A frock she donned with pride,
Thought it would be her style guide,
But soon the seams did shout,
'This isn't what it's about!'

With each step, a fabric tear,
She danced without a single care,
The dress flailed, twirled, and spun,
Laughter rose, oh what fun!

She wore a crown of mismatched flair,
A tiara from the local fair,
With sparkles shining all wrong,
The night sang a silly song!

In a world where glam might blind,
Real joy is hard to find,
So she learned to just let go,
And wear her laugh as a glow!

Unspoken Deceptions

A tale spun of stylish lies,
With money spent to mesmerize,
She flashed bling like a star,
But her wallet whispered, 'Bizarre!'

Friends noticed the shiny charade,
'Is that real?' they boldly paraded,
She faked a smile, played her part,
While her budget begged, 'Be smart!'

Each dinner date was a joke,
'Oh, this old thing?' she'd poke,
Until one day a slip revealed,
Her charm was less than sealed!

Now she grins with honest glee,
In thrift shop finds, she's truly free,
Who needs jewels that shine so bright?
A sense of humor fits just right!

Reflections in Gold

She thought she'd found pure gold,
In a bargain bin, so bold,
The shiny charm made her twirl,
'Look at me, I rule the world!'

But on closer inspection, oh dear,
It was plated, not sincere,
Her dreams of riches fell apart,
As giggles filled her beating heart!

Every day, she'd wear the shimm'r,
Her friends called it a big glimmer,
"Oops, is that a piece of foil?"
Laughter turned her anxiety to a boil!

In the end, she found her way,
With joy in treasures, come what may,
For life's greatest sparkles unfold,
From shared laughs, not just pure gold!

Chains of Enchantment

A sparkly charm hangs so fine,
But oh dear, it's just cheap twine!
She wears it with such grand delight,
While the truth sits, hidden from sight.

In parties, she dazzles, they all cheer,
But in her heart, she's filled with fear.
What if it frays or starts to break?
The jokes they'd tell, oh what a mistake!

With laughter loud, her jewels shine bright,
Yet, in the dark, they lose their light.
A twist of fate, it's all for show,
What will her friends say? They'll never know!

So here she stands, a queen of jest,
In an outfit full of fancy fest.
She giggles, slips, but never falls,
Chains of make-believe enthrall us all!

An Oath of Glamour

In a mirror, she vows with flair,
An oath of glam and fancy wear.
But the sparkles? Just glitter glue,
Adorning her neck like morning dew.

With a wink, she saunters down the street,
Every onlooker thinks she's neat.
But in her bag, she hides the truth,
A plastic gem, not one bit smooth!

"Look at me, I'm rich!" she sings,
While in reality, her dress just clings.
With laughter, her friends join the game,
"Who knew your glamour was all in the name?"

A sparkle here, a twinkle there,
Such audacity in the thin air.
They laugh along, oh what a sight,
Her oath of glam, their pure delight!

Shattered Illusions

A glimmer caught in a fleeting glance,
But what a trick, not true romance!
She holds it dear, a treasure bright,
Yet all it holds is a plastic bite.

In light, it shines like gold anew,
But shadows reveal the color blue.
"Oh darling, it's vintage!" she will lie,
But truth be told, it's all on the fly.

Her friends all gasp, "What a design!"
Yet she just smiles, sipping her wine.
When it shatters, oh what a scene,
"Just a prop," she laughs, "for my queen routine!"

With every click, the tales unfold,
Her shattered dreams, a story bold.
Yet laughter rings, a joyful sound,
In shattered illusions, joy is found!

The Art of Deceit

A clever clasp, a golden sheen,
In a world that's rarely seen.
With every step, she struts with glee,
Yet the truth? It's only make-believe.

"Oh darling, look at my lovely find!"
She beams, with charm and humor aligned.
Unbeknownst to all is a hidden truth,
Her glimmer is from a party booth.

As she spins tales, the crowd stays rapt,
Her art of deceit, a canvas untapped.
"Is it from Paris?" they all inquire,
She chuckles, "That's right, I must inspire!"

With every wink, she weaves her spell,
Creating stories, all quite swell.
In the art of deceit, she finds her place,
A laughter shared, a silly face!

The Illusion of Elegance

In a box that glitters so bright,
A treasure sparkles, a pure delight.
Yet, in the mirror, the truth unfurls,
A simple trinket for common girls.

With borrowed feasts and grand smiles wide,
She walks with poise, a graceful guide.
But laughter echoes, the humor in sting,
For elegance rests on a well-tied string.

The guests are dazzled, they raise a toast,
Yet whispers float of the dear, lost boast.
In the end, the glam fades like mist,
Was it a jewel or a mad prank twist?

All day she played, in her glittery guise,
Spinning tall tales, oh what a surprise!
In the end, she learns with a chuckle so bright,
True charm is laughter, not diamonds in sight.

Dusk's Gleaming Lies

At dusk she twirled in a dress so grand,
With sparkling bits that were slightly less planned.
She danced so high, with a glorious grin,
Yet underneath, the truth brewed within.

The friends all gasped, what a lovely sight!
Little did they know, it was quite a flight.
For pearls were painted, and diamonds too,
A whirlwind of lies, just to get through.

In the fancy light, they all took a peek,
Admiring a look that was just not unique.
Behind the glam, one slip and a wink,
Oh, the truth surfaced quicker than you think!

In the end, they laughed, a merry crew,
For elegance isn't just sparkles anew.
It's laughter, it's joy, and a dash of the bare,
Who needs the jewels when you've got good flair?

A Shimmering Betrayal

With a flick of her wrist, she wore a fake crown,
The glimmering trap made her slightly let down.
Oh, but the gala, it sparkled with tricks,
As secrets glittered like old magic tricks.

She spoke with flair, her stories so tall,
Of her travels grand, and her fortune's call.
Yet, in the shade of a gossip's parade,
The truth broke forth, a shimmering charade.

Gleaming jewels didn't match her routine,
It seemed her elegance was just a machine.
But laughter erupted, as stories unwound,
For betrayal was sweet when humor's around.

What good is a pearl if it's all just a lie?
In the end, it's the laughs that surely fly high.
With good friends beside, and a tale that's a laugh,
The shimmering truth was her best autograph.

Specters of Style

In the dim light, her cloaks they swayed,
With every shimmer, a mystery played.
Oh, the tales spun like a spider's web,
Of elegance worn with a pinch of ebb.

Her friends were entranced by the sparkling scene,
A specter of style in a glamorous sheen.
Yet whispers danced, jokes floated around,
As the night grew older, absurdities found.

"Is that a diamond or just a glass bead?
What's fancy, really? A falsehood, indeed!"
They chuckled and guffawed, the mood a delight,
For who needs the real when the fun feels just right?

So she twirled and she laughed, the night took its course,
With spectral style and an unstoppable force.
In the end, it's not about jewels or gold,
But revels and laughter that never grow old.

Mystique of a Trinket

A sparkly gem caught her eye,
She claimed it without a sigh.
Proudly she wore it, felt like a queen,
Unaware it was fake, not what it seemed.

With every party, she'd flaunt and boast,
Telling tall tales, like a ghost.
But the truth bubbled much too hot,
When it turned green - oh, what a plot!

Her friends giggled, 'Oh what a sight!'
As she scrubbed it with all her might.
'Next time,' she thought, 'I'll take more care,'
At least it made for a fun affair!

Radiance and Ruin

Dazzling beads around her neck,
A shimmer that screamed 'what the heck!'
She danced like a star, never a fool,
Till one broke loose - and made a pool.

With every step, a jingle rang,
Her laughter echoed - oh how it sang!
But soon enough, her spree would end,
As a cat dashed by, her only friend.

Lost treasures scattered far and wide,
Her necklace now a comic ride.
From fancy to frantic, the tale did shift,
Who knew jewels could cause such a rift?

The Lure of Luxury

Oh, to own the grand and fine,
She saved her pennies, made them shine.
When at last she hoped to spend,
The shopkeeper smirked - 'It's just pretend!'

With each shiny piece, joy turned to dread,
Wearing a fantasy spun in her head.
Every glance felt like a show,
But reality laughed - 'What a low blow!'

She wore it to brunch, feeling so grand,
Till it slipped from her grasp, like it planned.
A crash, a clatter, her heart full of fright,
Turns out luxury is not always right!

In Shadows of Splendor

In shadows deep, a shimmer glowed,
She thought it was gold, oh how it flowed!
With dreams of grandeur, she strutted forth,
Only to learn its true heavy worth.

'Where's the sparkle?' her friends would jest,
As the truth unraveled, it felt like a test.
Her once-shiny charm now a dull brown,
Made her giggle as she flopped down.

She swore off jewels, at least for now,
A reminder of folly, took a vow.
But laughter still echoed, rich and clear,
In shadows of splendor, she'd volunteer!

The Price of Vanity

In a shop, she did gleam,
With jewels that did beam,
She laughed at the price,
Thinking herself so nice.

The dress was a sight,
But oh, what a fright,
When she tripped on her gown,
And fell with a frown.

She posed for the crowd,
So happy, so loud,
Yet all they could see,
Was her shoe on a tree.

Her friends all did snicker,
As her pride grew thicker,
But vanity's game,
Is always the same.

Fragments of a Dream

She dreamt of a ball,
With gowns that enthrall,
Dancing under bright lights,
In shimmery sights.

But the dance turned to chaos,
As she lost the main focus,
Her gown split with a sound,
And left her spellbound.

The laughter rang clear,
As she drank too much beer,
Her tiara askew,
Oh, what a hullabaloo!

With sequins galore,
And not one person bore,
The weight of their dreams,
In their rhinestone schemes.

Lost in Opulence

A party of flair,
With chandeliers rare,
She wore all the bling,
Like a queen, or a king.

But her purse was a weight,
Full of items sedate,
With lipsticks galore,
And snacks she adored.

She tried to look fine,
In her dress that did shine,
But slipped on her heels,
And rolled like a wheel.

With crumbs on her chin,
She laughed with a grin,
"Opulence, oh my!
But I still can't fly!"

The Burden of Beauty

She bloomed with great grace,
In a sparkly lace,
But under the weight,
Of beauty, not fate.

Her friends did implore,
"Just settle the score,
But high heels are such pain,
Will you dance in the rain?"

A hairdo so wild,
She felt like a child,
Until wind made it fray,
"Who needs a bouquet?"

Yet beauty, it seems,
Is woven with dreams,
In laughter, we find,
What's silly and blind!

Secrets Woven in Silk

In a box of velvet dreams,
Lies a tale that gleams.
Oh, what a tangled web we weave,
When fashion tricks us to believe.

A lady lost in sparkling plight,
Chasing whims by day and night.
Her jewels are a joke, oh dear,
For laughter is the true veneer.

But under layers of fancy flair,
She finds joy beyond compare.
Each twinkle tells a silly tale,
Of what we chase, yet often fail.

So wear your charm, embrace the light,
And dance with glee, it's pure delight!
For in the end, it's not the bling,
But the laughter that makes our hearts sing.

Luster and Lies

A mirror sparkled, reflecting pride,
But oh, the truth we try to hide!
With every shimmer, a giggle or sneeze,
As carefree souls barter with ease.

She wore a crown of diamond dreams,
Yet found her luck bursting at the seams.
Each gem was brighter than it seemed,
As laughter spilled, unplanned and creamed.

In every pose, a wink, a grin,
Pretending gold when it's made of tin.
For life's too short to fret and frown,
Put on your smile, and paint the town!

Luster and lies twine in a dance,
Foolish moments, a vintage romance.
Let humor twinkle in your eyes,
And wear your truth in your disguise.

The Hidden Charm

In a dusty drawer, treasures bide,
With secrets hidden, they will not hide.
A brooch with stories, a fainted laugh,
Each glimmer holds a part of the path.

A funny twist, fate's silly plan,
Playing dress-up with a frying pan!
For what we crave is not the style,
But the joy that makes us pause and smile.

With baubles borrowed from old friends,
Gossip flows where laughter blends.
In sparkling wraps, we share our tales,
Of the mishaps where humor prevails.

So find your charm, let it shine bright,
In the dance of life, take delight.
For each piece tells a memory sweet,
And isn't that the real treat?

Echoes of Adornment

Beneath the sparkles, laughter rings,
A million echoed, joyful flings.
The jests we tell with blinged-out flair,
As friendships weave magic in the air.

Oh, the weight of jewels, heavy and bold,
Yet it's the laughter that never grows old.
For stories shared 'round gathered lights,
Bring more joy than any fancy sights.

Draped in pearls, their sheen so bright,
Fashion faux pas, a comedic sight.
In every twist of fabric fine,
Laughter's thread is the sweetest line.

Echoes of adornment glide on by,
With silly grins and a wink of an eye.
So wear your heart, let the jest begin,
For in the end, that's where the joy's pin.

Brilliance Behind Bars

Once a lady sought a spark,
Dressed in jewels, oh so stark.
But in her quest to shine so bright,
She lost her way in the moonlight.

With fancy gems that stole the show,
She strutted high, oh what a glow!
But little did she understand,
Her glamour trapped by fate's own hand.

A laughable dance in a borrowed dress,
She twirled and spun, oh what a mess!
For every twinkle brought a frown,
As she slipped and fell, plot twist abound.

Now in the mirror, what does she see?
A shimmering dream, a tragedy!
The jewels still shine, but hold on tight,
For the journey's tale is a comical sight.

The Glamour of Guilt

In the spotlight, she played the muse,
With borrowed bling and borrowed shoes.
She smiled wide, her heart a race,
But shadows whispered of her braced face.

Laughter echoed through the lavish halls,
As champagne poured and excitement calls.
Each clink of glass, a secret thought,
Would she get caught, or not?

But the truth's a joker, hiding in wait,
With a punchline tied to her gilded fate.
As drama unfurls in a pearl-studded jest,
The glamour turns to guilt, oh what a test!

With each new friend, a wink and a grin,
Her fortune's charm felt like a sin.
The irony tickled, a twisty delight,
In the game of laughter, who'd win this night?

Secrets on Display

Amidst the glitz, a secret bloomed,
A tale of riches, that left her doomed.
With every gaze, oh so divine,
She winked at fortune with a stolen shine.

Dressed to impress, she laughed with glee,
But chaos loomed, as all could see.
The truth played hide and seek on stage,
While she danced wildly, escaping from rage.

Each glance, a twist in her grand charade,
Bedazzled laughter paved her parade.
But whispers danced, and rumors swirled,
Her secrets on display, unfurled.

Through the tempest of glam, her light was lost,
In the laughter's echo, she counted the cost.
The curtain fell, and with it, the thrill,
Her secret still shimmered against her will.

Facets of Fate

In a soirée where laughter rang,
She showed off jewels and began to fang.
With every wink, the guests would cheer,
Oblivious to the fate lurking near.

A purse stuffed full of borrowed dreams,
Her sparkle turned into quirky schemes.
While tales of grandeur made faces grin,
Her heart raced fast as a whirlwind spin.

But fate's a trickster, playing along,
It twirled her jewels to its own song.
With every laugh, a plot would twist,
The glam turned silly, she couldn't resist.

Then came the moment, a slip, a slide,
Her borrowed beauty took quite a ride.
In a fit of giggles, she faced the crowd,
For the facets of fate were funny and loud.

Hidden Allure

In a box, it gleamed, oh so bright,
A trinket to charm, a sheer delight.
But oh dear friend, it had a twist,
From thrift shop finds, you get the gist.

You wore it proud, a sight to see,
Charmed all around, even the bee.
Yet at the end of the dazzling night,
You tripped, and it took off in flight!

A sparkly glow, a false parade,
A plastic gem, a grand charade.
But laughter echoed, a joyous buzz,
For truth in jest is still a plus.

So laugh along, don't take it hard,
For life's best jewels are often marred.
In humor born from silly bling,
You found the joy that laughter brings.

Whispers of Wealth

They whispered 'wealth', oh how they lied,
With glimmers of gold, they'd mock and bide.
But in the end, it lost its flair,
A shimm'ring joke, a plastic pair.

You strutted down, oh what a show,
Like riches flowed, with every glow.
Yet when the wind decided to play,
That shimmer danced and ran away!

Oh, dress it up, make it grand,
With every laugh, we understand.
That wealth is not in gems you wear,
But in the joy that's always there.

So clink and clatter, steal the show,
For laughter's worth much more, you know.
In every jest, a tale unwinds,
True wealth is found in merry minds.

The Mirage of Beauty

A lovely sight, it dazzled so,
Promising charm, a radiant glow.
But look a bit closer, don't be misled,
It's made of bits from the dollar spread!

You wore it high, with such great pride,
Yet whispers of truth would not subside.
Your friends would giggle, and point with glee,
For faux allure is beyond the spree!

Then came the night, the grand reveal,
When best-laid plans just felt unreal.
That glittering look fell to the floor,
And left you laughing, wanting more!

So in the end, it's all a phase,
To blink and cheer in mirthful blaze.
For beauty's grace can trick and tease,
But joy through folly comes with ease.

Laces of Longing

Adorned in glitz, you felt so fine,
With laces twinkled, all aligned.
Oh the longing to shine out bright,
Till it snagged a door and took a flight!

The party raged, the laughter soared,
But soon the eye began to hoard.
"What joy is this, a dance so bold,
If pieces fly, like tales retold?"

Yet every scoop of fleeting glimmer,
Set off a joy that made you shimmer.
In flimsy threads, you found the song,
The heart of laughter ever strong.

So laces frayed, do you still care?
For fun and folly dance in air.
In every twist of fate, it's clear,
The bonds of mirth are held most dear.

Stories in Gemstone

In a shop full of gems, quite a sight,
A woman lost in delight, oh what a fright.
She picked one so bright, thought it was gold,
Turned out to be glass, if the truth be told.

She wore it with pride, feeling so grand,
Whispers around her, oh wasn't it planned?
They laughed and they chuckled, what a bizarre scene,
Her royal appearance, so far from routine.

But in her own mind, she shone like a star,
While friends rolled their eyes, saying, "Look at her car!"
She danced through the night, gems shining with glee,
In her world of illusion, she was truly free.

The laughter erupted, she twirled all around,
Her sparkle, it seemed, could lighten the ground.
In the land of the funny, with friends by her side,
Stories in gemstone, she wore with such pride.

The Allure of Illusion

A gem so enticing, twinkling with mirth,
She claimed it was rare, of tremendous worth.
But her purse cried out, 'Honey, that's plastic!'
Yet she flaunted it fiercely, oh wasn't it drastic?

At parties she sparkled, a shimmering queen,
While the truth hid away, like it was unseen.
She'd laugh off the stares, 'Sweetness, it's all me!'
While friends shot each other a glancing spree.

In a realm of charades, she took center stage,
Her laughter a beacon, her joy all the rage.
Little did they know, under moon's gentle touch,
The allure was a ruse, but she loved it so much.

With giggles and winks, she played every part,
In her treasure of pretend, she just stole the heart.
So here's to delusions, they bring such delight,
The allure of illusion keeps everyone light.

A Dance of Dazzle

In a glittery ball, she stepped out with flair,
With jewels that sparkled, turning every stare.
But wait, what was that? A flicker of doubt,
A string of old lights, oh what a blowout!

She danced all around, with such whimsical glee,
Each twirl made the crowd holler, 'Look at her spree!'
The sparkle was grand, but in sunlight it waned,\nA twinkling assembly of façades uncontained.

With laughter infectious, she couldn't be stopped,
Claiming her kingdom till the laughter plopped.
"Behold my fine gems!" she declared with a cheer,
As they glimmered and winked, her confidence clear.

So let's toast to the dazzle, the bright and the bold,
With humor as armor, she jested, uncontrolled.
A dance of dazzle, a story so bright,
In the realm of the funny, she stole every light.

Threads of Deception

She draped herself in jewels, quite a sight,
With threads so questionable, but oh what a bite!
Claimed she was royal, from lands far away,
But her charm was the magic, come what may.

At brunch with the ladies, they stared in delight,
Adoring her stories, oh what sheer delight.
The truth laid beneath, a tangle of threads,
But they waved it away, tucked it under their heads.

With each sip of tea, tales spun like a web,
She painted adventures, each more than her ebb.
With each clink of her cup, laughter brewed high,
While her friends shared the joy, unaware of the lie.

In a world woven lightly with humor so grand,
Threads of deception made reality stand.
For in jest and in laughter, truth often leans,
She dazzled them all, a queen made of dreams.

Glistening Lies

She wore her shiny pearls with pride,
Yet borrowed them from a friend inside.
In the mirror, she'd posed grandly,
While her wallet felt quite scanty.

Her laughter rang like tiny bells,
As she spun tales, casting spells.
But a glance at her empty purse,
Surely was the universe's curse!

Oh what a night, full of flair,
With borrowed jewels and flowing hair.
Her friends just chuckled, couldn't resist,
As they planned their next winking twist!

In the end, the truth came clear,
Those shining gems were far from near.
Yet the joy of fun and laughter stayed,
A night of lies that never frayed!

Hidden Threads of Fate

She found a dress that fit just right,
But it was her sister's, quite a sight.
She danced and twirled without a care,
Unaware of the threadbare tear!

As fate would weave a giggling tale,
Her steps twisted, but she would not pale.
"Is that my shoe?" her sister cried,
As the crowd erupted, laughter amplified!

Turns out the dress had secrets too,
With pockets for snacks and a view askew.
A hidden stash of chips and cake,
Her sister's face was hard to fake!

By night's end, they shared a grin,
Amidst the chaos, fun did win.
For the threads of fate are wide and wacky,
Binding sisters, all things tacky!

Adorned Shadows

In an evening gown that sparkled and shone,
She glittered like the moon, yet felt all alone.
Her jewels were borrowed, lights were dim,
A stage for the charming, a clumsy whim!

With each step, she swayed and slipped,
Her shoe held secrets, the hem had ripped.
Laughter echoed off the wall,
As she made a spectacle, a grand faux pas call!

They crowned her queen of the party's mess,
A crown of flowers, no less!
"Fabulous!" they cheered, with a wink,
Who knew glamour involved inky ink?

In shadows of giggles, their fun took flight,
Her blunder turned into pure delight.
Adorned in laughter, she embraced the night,
Crowned by her friends, oh what a sight!

The Weight of Glamour

She strutted in heels that made her sway,
A cascade of jewels, come what may.
But with each step, her confidence dipped,
As the burden of glamour had her tripped!

Chandeliers sparkled like stars above,
She twisted and twirled, bestowing love.
Yet laughter erupted as jewels did fly,
A dazzling scatter, oh my, oh my!

Friends picked jewels from the ground with cheer,
"Oh look, another diamond, dear!"
They crowned her a jester, what a display,
In a night of symptoms, but less hooray!

Through the mayhem, she reveled in glee,
The weight of glamour set her free.
For in the laughter, she found her grace,
Glistening jewels, brightening the place!

www.ingramcontent.com/pod-product-compliance
Lightning Source LLC
Chambersburg PA
CBHW070320120526
44590CB00017B/2752